Perspectives
And Other Life Seasonings

Cathy Burnham Martin

Published and printed in the United States of America

QUIET THUNDER

www.QTPublishing.com

Quiet Thunder Publishing

Naples, FL   Manchester, NH   Columbus, NC

**This title and more can be found at
www.GoodLiving123.com**

Paperback edition: ISBN 978-0-9832136-4-2
eBook edition: ISBN 978-0-9770711-2-8
Audiobook edition: ISBN 978-0-9770722-8-0

Library of Congress Control Number: 2025914035

Perspectives
And Other Life Seasonings

Dedication

"Perspectives" is respectfully dedicated to my Northeastern University communications master's degree professors and cohorts, Class of 2009. Together we discovered new perspectives that helped us fly and reveled in age-old perspectives that kept us grounded.

They started my journey into publishing with me, as I started my Life Seasonings series in theory. It was just a little book of quotations that I made by hand for each of my classmates. Having completed twenty-four books in my new career, it is now time to finalize this book and officially launch the series.

Thanks, my friends, for all your energy, dedication, and thoughtfulness.

Cathy

Foreword

As part of my ongoing research in life, I continually seek out and collect quips, quotations, words of wisdom, serious thoughts, and humorous tidbits. These "Notable Quotables" hail from all walks of life, the famous and the lesser known, both modern and classically aged. I share some of these gems to add sparkle to our thinking and support in times when harmony is deeply needed.

> *"Blessed is he who expects nothing,*
> *for he shall never be disappointed."*
> --Jonathan Swift (1667 – 1745)
> Irish writer, satirist, & political theorist

(Photo by Nadine E. Shaabana)

I believe it always helps to step back, pause, and find calmness. We can examine our lives, activities, influences, and circumstances to better understand how we reached our perspectives, attitudes, and viewpoints in the first place.

> *"We don't see things as they are.*
> *We see them as <u>we</u> are."*
> --Anaïs Nin (1903 – 1977)
> French-American writer

May we always respect our perspectives and those of others. May our constant evolution continue.

Table of Contents

Dedication   v
Foreword   vii

1 Embracing Differences   1

2 Values   7

3 Attitudes   15

4 Considering Other Viewpoints   23

5 Positioning   31

6 Questioning and Changing   41

7 Taking Action   53

8 Practicing Mindfulness   65

9 In Closing   77

Photography Credits   79
About the Author   81
Other Titles   83
Partial List of Audiobooks
        Narrated by Cathy Burnham Martin   89

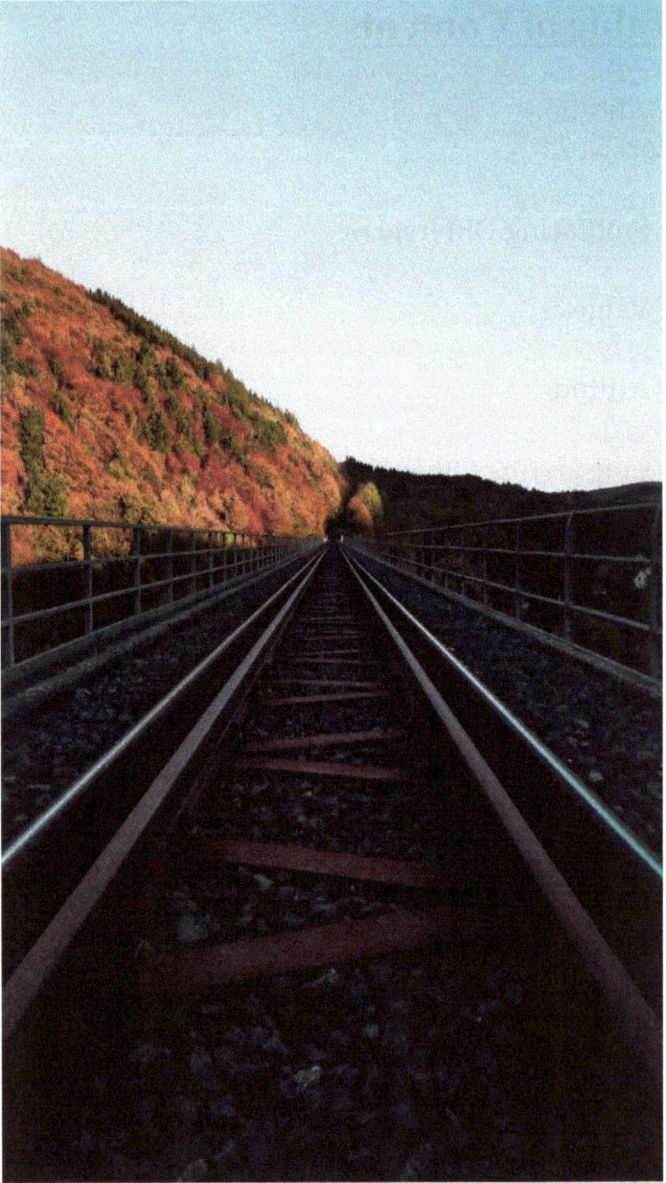

(Photo by Javid Naderi)

1

Embracing Differences

Likely, we all know both "can-do" and "can't do" people. Some people excitedly approach each new challenge with investigation, enthusiasm, and action. Some people whine at high speed, wringing their hands as they bemoan the awfulness with which they must somehow cope.

We are different from each other. So, we see things differently. We have various perspectives.

In my "Life Seasonings" series, we seek out more than the salt and pepper options. We season our lives with cool and fiery spices, savory and subtle herbs, citrusy and sweet flavors. Needs and tastes vary… just as perspectives do.

One viewpoint is not necessarily superior to another. The movers and shakers of the world came in all shapes, sizes, and attitudes.

"Perspectives" reflects on ways of considering all aspects of Life. Our points of view develop constantly.

(Photo by Viktor Mindt)

Whether we like it or admit it… or not, each one of us has full control over how we choose to view Life. We can choose wisely… or not. But we are in charge of our thoughts, opinions, and responses to those who feel differently.

What one person swears is pure fact, another is equally confidant reigns as pure fiction. The back-and-forth banter sometimes turns brutal. Loud and ferocious diatribes are hurled from every corner. Vital is developing the strength to not let naysayers

"The gem cannot be polished without friction,
nor man perfected without trials."

--Chinese proverb

When someone we know and love expresses distress or rage over our differing opinions, it saddens us, at best. At worst, it shakes us to the core.

We may have tried to gently share our differing thoughts. We may have strongly debated them and powerfully advocated our stance. We also may have remained quiet, opting to avoid conflict.

"No one can make you feel inferior without your consent. Never give it to them."

--Eleanor Roosevelt (1884 – 1962)
Former First Lady of the U.S., diplomat & activist

Through social media and in my daily GoodLiving123.com articles, I attempt to present positive and thoughtful postings and timely quotations. While the vast majority of comments are affirming and filled with gratitude, I have felt deeply saddened by a couple of friends I have known for many years.

(Photo by Melissa Askew)

When anyone else offers a statement or position with which they disagree, particularly regarding politics, their anger crackles and roars as if fueled by an out-of-control forest fire. There is nothing logical, never mind factual, that can be shared to help them dial it down a few notches.

They may rant as if it is their sworn duty to save everyone who believes differently than they do, without the slightest consideration that their attitude and reactions alone indicate that they may well be in need of saving.

Some people have decided that their opinions and thoughts are the only legitimate ones. We can do our best by learning not to take it to heart.

(Photo by Meg Aghamyan)

*"The greater the difficulty,
the greater the glory."*

--Cicero (Marcus Tullius Cicero) (106 BC – 43 BC)
Roman statesmen & attorney

I choose to edify people, regardless of their negative or divisive rantings. I do this by making and sharing comments that tend to make people nod their heads in compliance. I smile as I read all the "likes" and agreements posted... even from friends that I know hail from distinctly different schools of thought or sides of the political aisle. When we can inspire people on both sides of a polarizing argument to agree enthusiastically with something, then we are saying something right.

We are seeking shared perspectives. The world is overflowing with them. Sharing positive thoughts and ideas strengthens everyone. We need not be afraid of the words or lyrics when we are delivering beautiful music. Truthfully, if we are going to walk on thin ice anyway, we might as well dance!

"Running away will never make you free."

--Kenny Loggins (1948 -)
American singer & songwriter

(Photo by Brett Jordan)

Wanting to do something well builds our courage. We develop sureness in our efforts when we know that we have the ability to do something well. But we must not be timid when it comes to moving forward, Confidence will be the result of getting the job done well.

Let's learn to appreciate and feel comfortable with our perspectives. If we are unsure or recognize that we may be on the wrong track, we can learn to see things differently.

Let us step forward by considering our values and social mores.

Values

2

<u>Values</u>

We all have beliefs, standards and ideals. These personal social mores shape our perspectives.

As children, we may well have had a more innocent viewpoint and approach to Life… if we were lucky and blessed with positive support at home. The passage of time, our experiences, and education continually shape our thinking.

"Better keep yourself clean and bright;
you are the window
through which you must see the world."

--George Bernard Shaw (1856 – 1950)
Irish playwright, critic, and political activist

(Photo by Gabriel Tenan)

As a child, Mom had some rules that were not debatable. She had learned them from her own mother. And neither one of them ever wavered on what they believed was right.

"You can make your bed with a smile,
or you can make your bed with a frown,
but you're going to make your bed."

--Glenna Burnham (1930 -)
My All-Time Great American Mother

As adults, we may knowingly or unknowingly become jaded or seemingly warped in some of our perspectives. However, we also have the ability to carefully consider *why* our viewpoints have taken on the shapes they have. Then we can also reconsider, review, and revise our thinking.

If you don't change your beliefs,
your life will be like this forever.
Is this good news?"

--Douglas Noel Adams (1952 – 2001)
English author & humorist

Our values and how we reached these beliefs result from a lifetime of weaving complex tapestries of threads, colors, and textures. We need to choose carefully and appreciate fully.

It has to be dark for the stars to appear.

Photo by Klemen Vrankar

We all have cognitive differences. For example, some of us seek wide-ranging information, while some only seek information that firmly validates our notions.

"I was seldom able to see an opportunity until it ceased to be one."

--Mark Twain (1835 – 1910)
(Pen name for Samuel Langhorne Clemens)
American writer and humorist

Regardless of our different backgrounds and life experiences, we may look at the same challenges from very different angles. Where our needs have and have not been met directly impacts our thought processes, reactions, and responses.

"The greater part of our happiness or misery depends on our dispositions and not our circumstances."

--Martha Dandridge Washington (1731 – 1802)
1st First Lady of the United States

Early foundations become our bedrock for how we perceive relationships, employment, family, authority figures, and so much more. Our development process can be slow. Challenges, road bumps, disappointments, and heartaches all continually play roles in attempts to dampen our spirits.

There are no shortcuts to any place worth going.

As we reflect on past experiences, we start to understand why we think the way we do. When we consider how the past has shaped our current perspective, we get to know our true inner character. We also can decide just where those experiences fit in our realm of relevance.

"Character is like a tree
and reputation a shadow.
The shadow is what we think of it;
the tree is the real thing."

--Abraham Lincoln (1809-1865)
American statesman; 16th President: 1861-65
Assassinated following Civil War

Our values reflect our personal selves, our families and friends, our neighbors, and everyone else with whom we come in contact. Values directly impact business, too. However, it is important to note that there is less to fear from outside competition than from inside inefficiency, discourtesy, negative attitudes, and bad service.

"The measure of success is not whether you
have a tough problem to deal with, but whether
it's the same problem you had last year."

--John Foster Dulles (1888 – 1959)
American lawyer, diplomat
& former U.S. Secretary of State

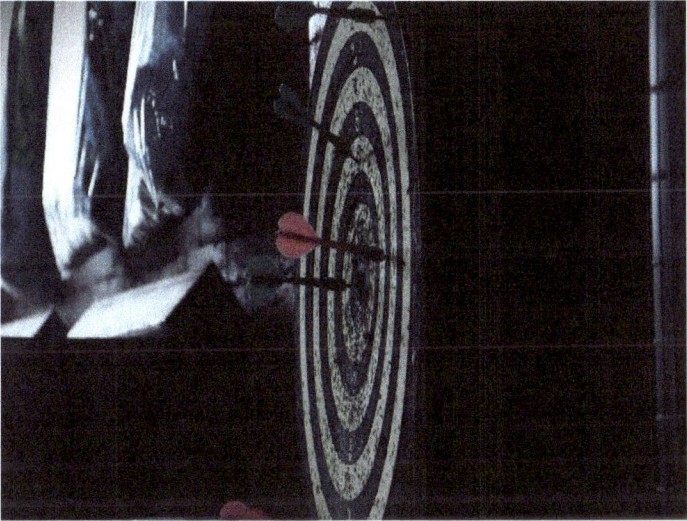

*"Define your business goals clearly so that
others can see them as you do."*

--George F. Burns (1947 -)
American litigator and business advisor

As our comfort level grows with our values, our perspectives, and our evolving attitudes, we become better people. This applies seamlessly to our private and professional lives. The more people respect our personal fairness, calmness, and sensibility, the more they can dare to do the same in their own lives.

(Photo by Felipe Bastias)

By sharing or "paying it forward," we are helping others to become their best selves. This builds teams in the most powerful ways. Remember, the best teamwork has us working together, even when we're apart.

"We have learned that power is a positive force if it is used for positive purposes."

--Elizabeth Dole (1936 -)
American attorney, author, and US Senator

3

Attitudes

Traumas can make a person more pessimistic, even hopeless. And yet, the very same traumas can develop in another person the strength to stand up and strive to do better, despite parallel negative circumstances.

> *"What optimists and pessimists*
> *have in common*
> *is that they both think they are realists.*
> *And they're both right!"*

--Ted McDonald (1891 – 1937)
Tasmanian cricketer

*"If you ever get
a second chance in life for something,
you've got to go all the way."*

--Lance Armstrong (1971 -)
American road racing cyclist

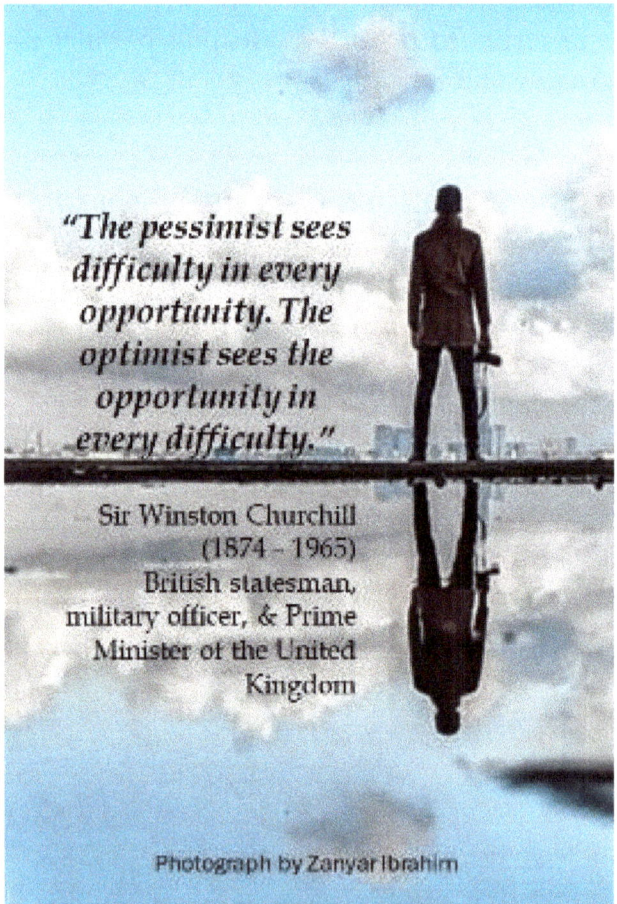

"The pessimist sees difficulty in every opportunity. The optimist sees the opportunity in every difficulty."

Sir Winston Churchill
(1874 - 1965)
British statesman,
military officer, & Prime
Minister of the United
Kingdom

Photograph by Zanyar Ibrahim

"If you don't like
something, change it.
If you can't change it,
change your attitude."

-- Maya Angelou
(1928 – 2014)
American memoirist,
poet, and activist

*"The last of the human freedoms
is to choose one's attitudes."*

--Viktor Frankl (1905 – 1997)
Austrian neurologist, psychologist, philosopher, &
Holocaust survivor

When reality seems too negative to bear, it helps to let ourselves dream and bring hope closer to fruition. It has often been said that to those who can dream, there is no such place as far away.

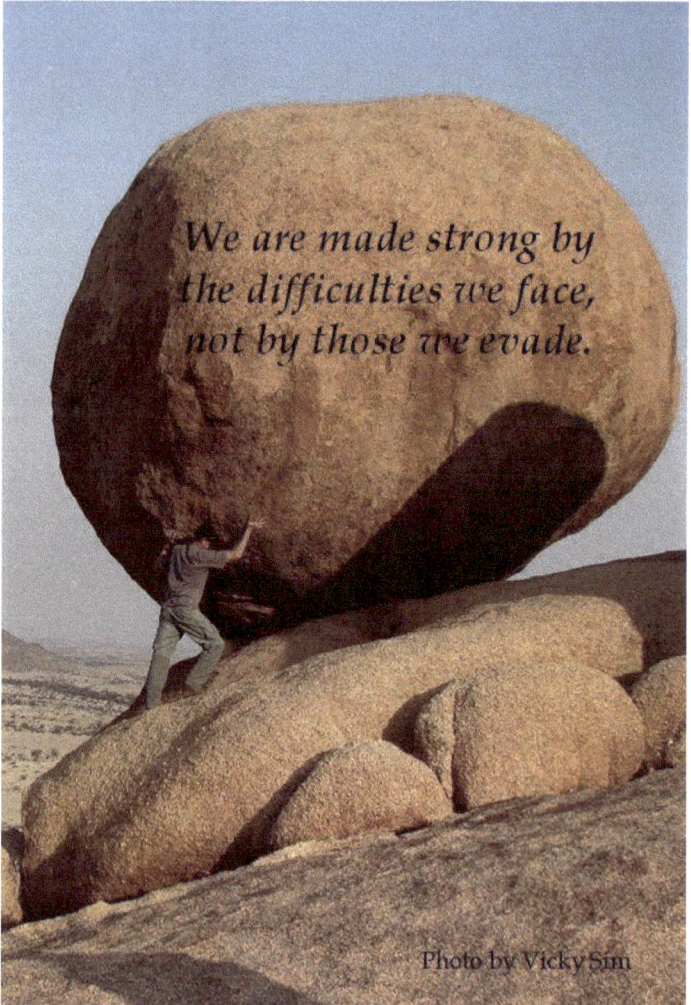

We are made strong by the difficulties we face, not by those we evade.

Photo by Vicky Sim

"It is wise to keep in mind that neither success nor failure is ever final."

--Roger Babson (1875 – 1967)
American economist

Two people can listen to the same exact news report and have completely different reactions. One feels confident that the needed actions will be taken, and everything will work out.

The other starts running around as if the sky was falling, and doom was upon us. The bottom line includes the fact that we are not in charge. Often, what happens in life is not as important as how we accept it.

"I have not failed. I've just found 10,000 ways that won't work."

--Thomas Edison (1847 – 1931)
American inventor & businessman

*"Great effort springs
naturally from great attitude."*

--Pat Riley ((1945 -)
American NBA player & coach

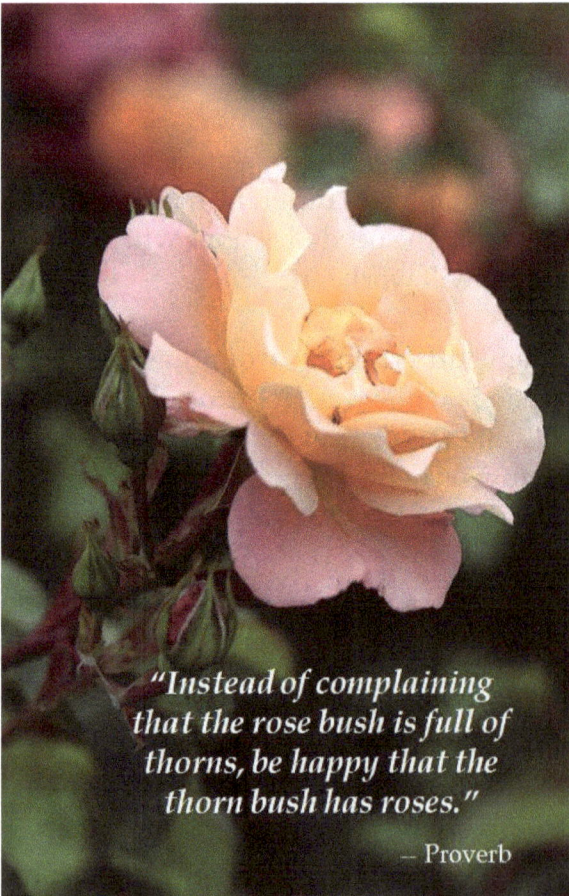

*"Instead of complaining
that the rose bush is full of
thorns, be happy that the
thorn bush has roses."*

– Proverb

Past experiences mold our prejudices, biases, and pre-conceived notions. In essence Life teaches us our perspectives. This ongoing process finds both positive and negative interactions continually shaping and reshaping our thinking.

"Do not let what you cannot do
interfere with what you can do."

--John Wooden (1910 – 2010)
American basketball coach & player

Our peer groups, social circles and the volumes of media we consume further develop our many perspectives. This often happens without us even realizing it. Our perspectives evolve rapidly or gradually, depending on internal and external factors.

"If you aren't fired with enthusiasm,
you will be fired with enthusiasm."

--Vince Lombardi (1913 – 1970)
American NFL football coach

To lead fuller lives with broader perspectives, it helps to identify our own negative thoughts. Recognizing that we may participate in negative self-talk is important. Once we realize what we are doing, we can better understand that we are limiting our own beliefs. This alone may also be influencing our perspective.

"Success is the ability to go from failure to failure without losing your enthusiasm."

--Winston Churchill (1874 – 1965)
British statesman, military officer,
& Prime Minister of the United Kingdom

4

Considering Other Viewpoints

No one wants to be thought of as close-minded. We prefer to think of ourselves as objective, thoughtful, and open-minded. We do not like being told what to do, never mind how to think or feel. We want to consider all the information and come to our own conclusions or draw our own perspectives.

> *"Never tell people how to do things.*
> *Tell them what to do*
> *and they will surprise you*
> *with their ingenuity."*
>
> -- George S. Patton, Jr. (1885 – 1945)
> American General in U.S. Army

Being too open-minded can lead us to a point where we may become unable to discriminate between sense and nonsense. We may be putting our heart in front of our head. If we jump on every ideological bandwagon that rolls around, we may be gullible, if not ignorant. At best we are easily confused and could even lose our ability to make critical judgments.

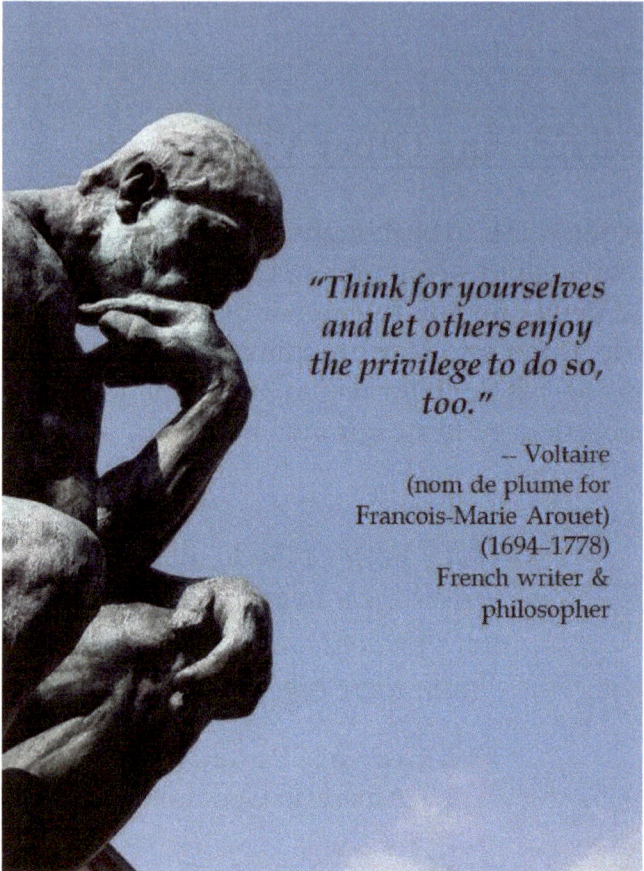

> *"Think for yourselves
> and let others enjoy
> the privilege to do so,
> too."*
>
> — Voltaire
> (nom de plume for
> Francois-Marie Arouet)
> (1694–1778)
> French writer &
> philosopher

However, if we are too close-minded, we end up drawing strong conclusions without getting all the facts. We may focus on disapproving of and disproving others, rather than finding fresh perspectives and informational clarification. Closing our minds is a powerful way of holding ourselves back. We lead ourselves to a lack of intellectual and personal growth.

"Too many people miss the silver lining because they're expecting gold."

--Maurice Setter (1936 – 2020)
English football (soccer) player & manager

(Photo by Jonny Clow)

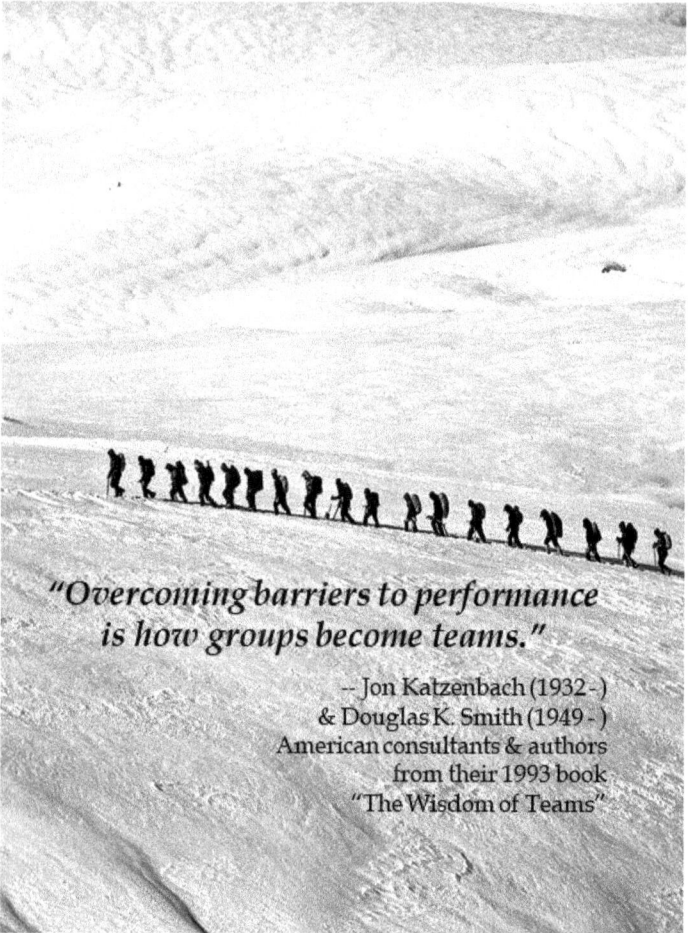

"Overcoming barriers to performance is how groups become teams."

-- Jon Katzenbach (1932 -)
& Douglas K. Smith (1949 -)
American consultants & authors
from their 1993 book
"The Wisdom of Teams"

*"No one can whistle a symphony.
It takes an orchestra to play it."*

--Halford E. Luccock (1885 – 1960)
American Methodist minister and professor

"There is more hunger for love and appreciation in this world than for bread."

--Mother Teresa (1910 – 1997)
Albanian Indian Roman Catholic nun & saint

Considering other viewpoints strengthens us and the perspectives we hold. Only when we genuinely empathize with others are we truly listening to them and trying to understand another person's perspective without judgment.

This requires time, thoughtfulness, and caring. We all can attempt to fully ponder the relevance of someone else's background, experiences, thoughts, feelings, and motivations.

"Since we cannot change reality, let us change the eyes which see reality."

--Nikos Kazantzakis (1833 – 1957)
Greek writer & journalist

Even if we think they are far off base, seeking diverse opinions helps us learn. We do not have to change our own beliefs. We might, but we might not.

After engaging with people who hold different viewpoints, listening fully, and being open to learning from them, we may add to our own perspective. We may change our mind completely.

We could just as easily end up feeling more confident in our original position. Better yet, we even have new data and alternate perspectives to strengthen our viewpoint.

Think about the times we start reading a friend's posting on a social media site. Soon we realize, it's not a posting, but rather, it's a full-out rant. They are vehement, angry, unstoppable, and certainly not open to input or other thoughts.

Generally, I choose not to engage them in any back-and-forth conversation. I may offer a supportive comment to them as a person to let them know that I care that they are writhing in such a negative emotional state.

They have already made it crystal clear that they are not at all open-minded. So, I see no benefit to invest a great deal of time torturing either one of us by trying to help them consider the validity in any other line of thinking. I may feel deeply saddened by their frustrated state of mind. I may deeply wish I could help to open their heart and mind. I pray for calmness and light to reach them.

> *"When the power of love overcomes the love of power, the world will know peace."*
>
> -- Jimi Hendrix (1942 – 1970)
> American singer, songwriter, & musician

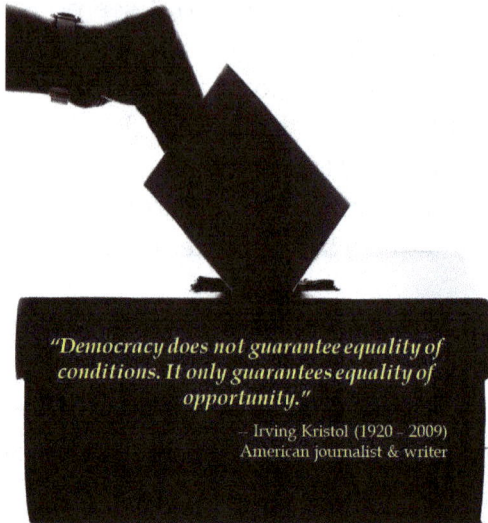

"Democracy does not guarantee equality of conditions. It only guarantees equality of opportunity."

– Irving Kristol (1920 – 2009)
American journalist & writer

I turn the page. I am not suggesting we abandon people we recognize need help.

However, I prefer to gently hug those with defiantly closed minds and hearts. I respect people with opinions that are diametrically opposed to my own, even when they insist that they speak the facts, and I must be crazy. Regardless, I feel no obligation to make them open or change their minds.

Instead, I choose to focus the majority of my time and efforts on those who wish to grow and resound with positivity and hope. Differing opinions and perspectives are fine.

5

<u>Positioning</u>

Often, if we change our physical position, our view changes our perspective, too. Seeing physical things from different angles changes everything and broadens our viewpoint.

Imagine looking at a tree while standing on your head. Or looking at a flower from the side versus from on top. A different angle gives a very different view. Issues in life are not so different.

We gain very different
perspectives when we
look down,
stand on the ground
and look straight on,
or look straight up.

If you have been in a plane, you know how cities, meadows, pastures, rivers, and even mountains appear when we look down on them. New patterns seem to emerge.

A skyscraper looks lovely from the air, but it becomes towering when we stand on a sidewalk beside it and look up. The building did not change. Our perspective changed and made all the difference.

When I started college as a theatre major with a commercial art minor, I was thrilled to help draw and paint a perspective backdrop for a theatre production. We created a street scene, which, when viewed by the audience, added depth to the stage, giving the illusion that the street continued behind the actors on the stage.

Called "perspective drawing," close-up buildings are larger at the outer edges, shrinking toward to center to appear further back.

Physical perspectives can be far easier to perceive than points of view. Sometimes when it seems most difficult to see or comprehend things clearly, we can get quite easily frustrated. This is totally understandable.

Don't get discouraged. We need to remind ourselves that it's usually the last key in the bunch that opens the lock. While that quip sounds rather wry, the fact is that we stop looking once we find a key that works. By default, that key becomes the last key.

(Photo by Conny Schneider)

A misty morning does not signify a cloudy day.

Photo by Micah Bratt

We all have days that start out badly. That does not have to mean that the entire day is ruined. Needing positive reminders is perfectly understandable and normal. Learning to accept them gratefully can hurry us along the path to positivity.

If we allow ourselves to change our perspective, we can deal with disappointments and negative changes and get positive results.

In fact, doing so is easier than staying sad or grumpy. Negative stress is exhausting.

(Photo by Daniel Lincoln)

An ageless expression says that if we growl all day, we'll feel dog tired all night. Grumbling and growling through our challenges will help absolutely no one. Worse yet, it frustrates and annoys everyone, including ourselves... whether we like to admit it or not.

"The universe is a big place.
But it's okay - you'll grow into it."

--Carl Munson (1936 -)
British Portuguese podcaster

When things are not going well, we can often make some simple changes and enjoy true improvement. Sometimes a basic change in our physical environment is all it takes to gain a brighter perspective.

"It is not the mountain we conquer,
but ourselves."

--Sir Edmund Hillary (1919 – 2008)
New Zealand mountaineer & explorer

Try moving to a new chair, room, or location. Or try a different activity for a change of pace. Often it helps to spend time with people who hold different perspectives, but only if they do so while also exuding positive outlooks.

Changing is the end of something, but it is also the beginning of something else. When we find ourselves in a dark, negative state of mind, change lets in the light.

(Photo by Suzanne D Williams)

"What the caterpillar calls the end, the rest of the world calls a butterfly."

--Lao Tzu (Laozi) (571BC – 5th Century BC)
Chinese philosopher

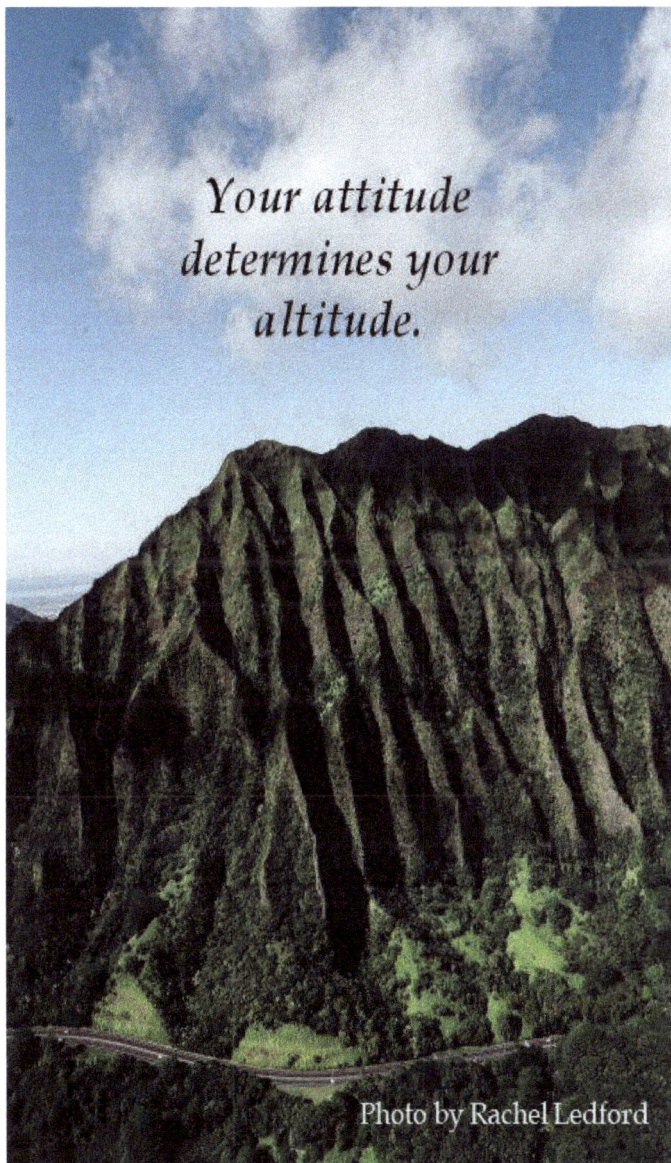

Your attitude
determines your
altitude.

Photo by Rachel Ledford

"Teams share the burden and divide the grief."

--Doug Smith (1964 -)
Canadian American ice hockey player

*"Let your hopes, not your hurts,
shape your future."*

--Robert H. Schuller (1926 – 2015)
American televangelist & author

*"Audacity, and again audacity,
and always audacity. "*

--G.J. Danton (1759 – 1794)
French lawyer, orator, and revolutionary

6

Questioning and Changing

Before change can have a chance at a solid foothold, we must believe that we need to change something about ourselves. If we sense or have been repeatedly told that we may be exuding negativity, that is typically hard to accept.

*"It's not the load that breaks you down;
it's the way you carry it."*

--Lena Horne (1917 – 2010)
American singer, actress, & dancer

When we are fortunate, we become inspired to question our own assumptions, even those we have held for as long as we can recall. This requires a full reckoning, so to speak. It could be somewhat like washing a window. Clarity is best achieved by washing the entire pane of glass, rather than dabbing at one obvious spot.

"We must change in order to survive."

--Pearl Bailey (1918 – 1930)
American actress & singer

Most everyone resists change because change brings the unknown. This is true. And yet, we can conquer our fears with trust and knowledge. Only by going through changes can we learn how resilient we really are.

*"Only I can change my life.
No one can do it for me."*

--Carol Burnett (1933 -)
American comedian, actress, singer, and writer

(Photo by Chris Lawton)

(Photo by Creed Ferguson)

"There is a crack in everything.
That's how the light gets in."

--Leonard Cohen (1934 – 2016)
Canadian songwriter

(Photo by Scott Higdon)

To change perspective, we intentionally shift our viewpoint or understanding of a situation. We do this through various means.

> *"To keep our faces toward change*
> *and behave like free spirits*
> *in the presence of fate,*
> *is strength undefeatable."*

--Helen Keller (1880 – 1968)
American author, lecturer, & political advocate

We might start by listening to or studying different viewpoints. Or we could attempt to change our own basic assumptions. We can dramatically help ourselves by actively seeking new information.

"Very often a change of self is needed more than a change of scene."

--Arthur Christopher Benson (1862-1925)
English essayist, poet, & academic

Let us review what we have been considering. A good starting point could be acknowledging and even challenging our current perspective. We all develop strong opinions. We become biased. We can start thinking that what we know is what everyone else should also know and believe.

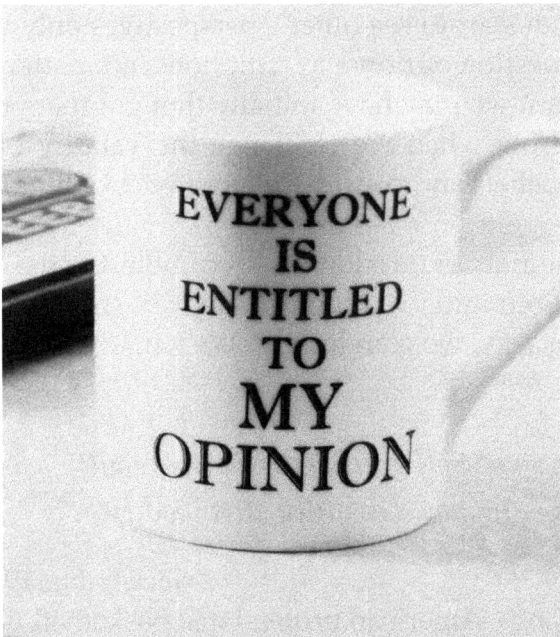

(Photo by Steve Johnson)

We can analyze and even put into words some of our own perspectives. This helps us to develop awareness of our innermost thoughts and feelings, as well as our initial reactions and assumptions about a situation, a feeling, or a current event.

*"In the middle of every difficulty
lies opportunity."*

--Albert Einstein (1879 – 1955)
German theoretical physicist

We can start to see other's perspectives only when we question our own assumptions, no matter how brilliant we may have initially thought them to be. We grow when we challenge the validity of our own beliefs and consider alternative explanations.

Our initial assumptions may crumble. On the other hand, our initial assumptions may be strengthened. Either way, we gain insight. We win.

*"Self-confidence is the result
of a successfully survived risk."*

--Jack Gibb (1995 -)
American professional basketball player

"The Wright brothers flew right through the smokescreen of impossibility."

– Charles F. Kettering (1876 – 1958)
American inventor & engineer

Photo by Sonny Maurico

All too often, we get down on ourselves, our friends, our circumstances, or our lives, in general. We may start spewing toxically negative words, phrases, concepts, and attitudes without even realizing the devastating impact such expressions can have.

(Photo by Danilo Alvesd)

We can and should challenge our own negative self-talk. We grow in amazingly awesome ways when we do something as basic as replace negative thoughts with decidedly positive affirmations and encouraging self-talk.

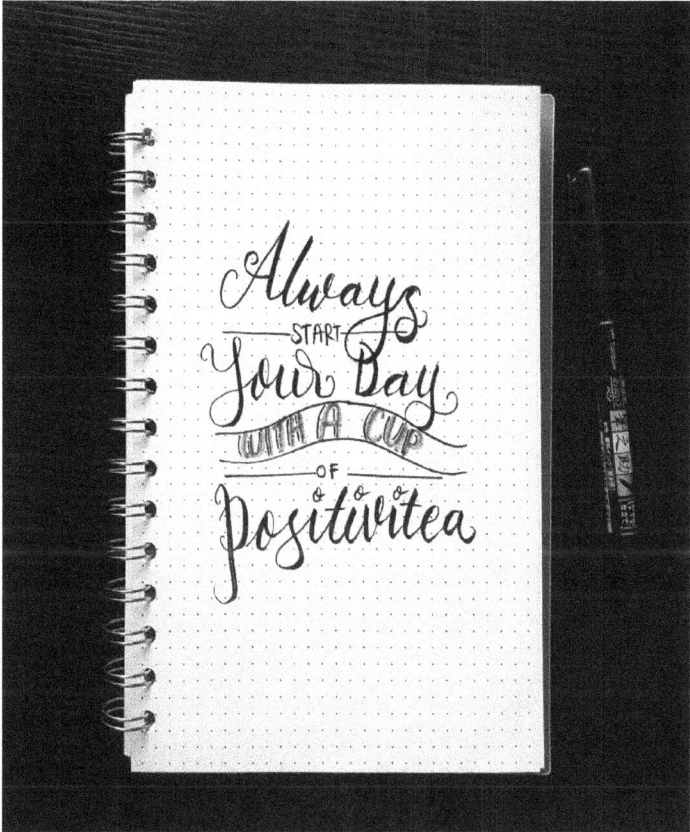

Considering the bigger picture always helps us gain a fuller and more positive outlook. We do this by stepping back and analyzing the situation from a broader perspective.

This includes considering long-term implications. As we seek awareness of our perspectives, we can study a multitude of external factors that constantly bombard us with information and disinformation.

The Internet and social media sites shower us with a barrage of images, ideas, facts, and opinions. Many other external forces remain in play also.

Things happen to us all day long. These experiences, whether they occur during work or play, with friends or family influence our perspectives.

Other external influences feed our thinking through current events, social norms, the environment, and even the music we hear.

Consider this. Has a song ever made you think? Or smile? Or even cry? We hear something unsettling in the news. We get worried, or sad, or even angry.

Things around us influence our thinking every hour of every day. This is happening whether we know it or not. Even the weather can influence our thinking and attitudes. Some of us are happy on bright, sunny days, but we may feel blah, if not sad, on dreary or stormy days.

There are many aspects of our perspectives that we instilled from the outside without our direct awareness, too. Consider a childhood upbringing. Life may have been supportive and positively foundational. Or experiences could have rained down a great deal of stress and negativity that had to be carefully maneuvered just to survive.

All family dynamics are different. Not all are positive. Not all are negative. Most include some portion of both.

Our experiences in youth developed our values. These perspectives were instilled by parents, caregivers, teachers, clergy members, or others who had influence over us.

Understanding factors that played roles in developing our perspectives helps us choose which ones we want upheld. This also guides us toward recognizing changes we may want to make in our own thinking.

(Photo by Renan Brun)

7

Taking Action

"Whenever you are asked if you can do a job,
tell 'em, 'Certainly, I can!'
Then get busy and find out how to do it."

-- Theodore "Teddy" Roosevelt (1858 – 1919)
26th U.S. President

For many reasons, taking action after making a decision becomes the hard part. In theory, we may clearly know how we think, what needs to happen, why we seek change, if we do.

Translating our decision into part of our actual world takes a great deal of discipline. If someone wants to do anything, one foot in front of the other is the way to get there. We cannot sing until we dare open our mouths and let it happen. We cannot dance if we sit still on the sidelines like wallflowers.

Voluntary motion is needed. Of course, a few things are blessedly involuntary. We cannot breathe unless we inhale. Thankfully, we do so by involuntary action. Our focus in this guide is on voluntary actions we can all choose to take.

*"Chaotic action
is preferable to orderly inaction."*

--Karl E. Weick (1936 -)
American psychologist

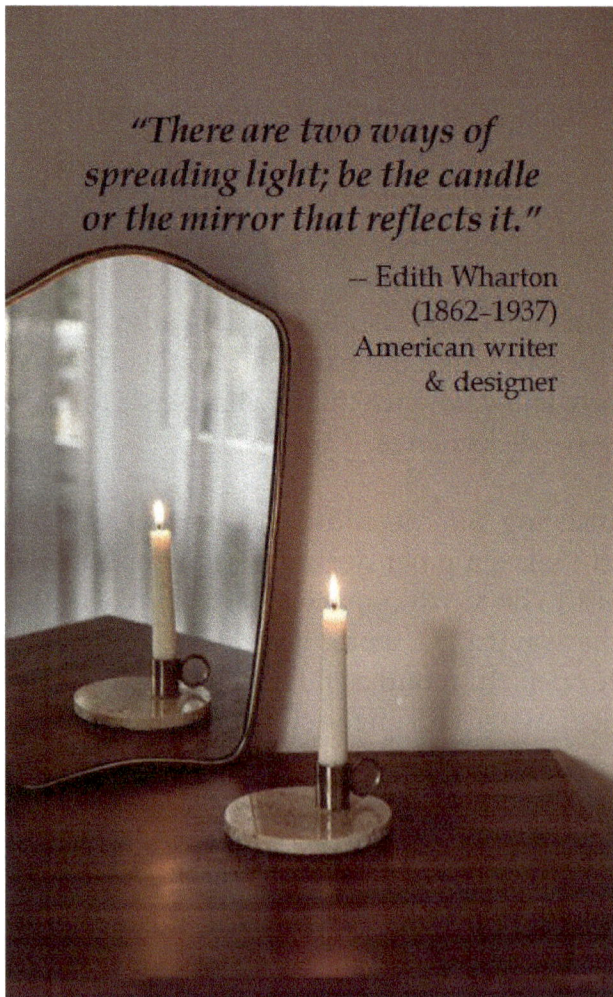

*"There are two ways of
spreading light; be the candle
or the mirror that reflects it."*

— Edith Wharton
(1862–1937)
American writer
& designer

"Do or do not. There is no try."

--Yoda
Fictional character in "Star Wars" franchise

*"The brain is a wonderful organ.
It starts working the moment
you get up in the morning,
and does not stop until you get into the office."*

-- Robert Frost (1874 – 1963)
American poet

*"It's not what they take away from you
that counts.
It's what you do with what you have left."*

--Hubert Humphrey (1911 – 1978)
American politician &
28th vice president of the U.S.

(Photo by Aziz Acharki)

*"If everything's under control,
you're going too slow."*

--Mario Andretti (1940 -)
American racing driver & businessmen

*"A wise man makes more opportunities
than he finds."*

--Francis Bacon (1561 – 1626)
English philosopher, statesman, & scientist

Why are there so many people who never miss an opportunity to miss an opportunity? I think it has a lot to do with self-esteem and self-confidence. We can feel so "down" on ourselves that we start seeing opportunities as wonderful hands up for other people. And yet, we may not feel worthy.

We most definitely need fresh perspectives. And we need them now. Tomorrow will not be any brighter unless we determine to make it so. There is no time like the present.

"Carpe diem." (Seize the day.)

--Horace (65 BC – 8 BC)
(pen name for Quintus Horatius Flaccus)
Roman poet

*"Opportunity is missed by most people because
it is dressed in overalls and looks like work."*

--Thomas Edison (1847 – 1931)
American inventor & businessman

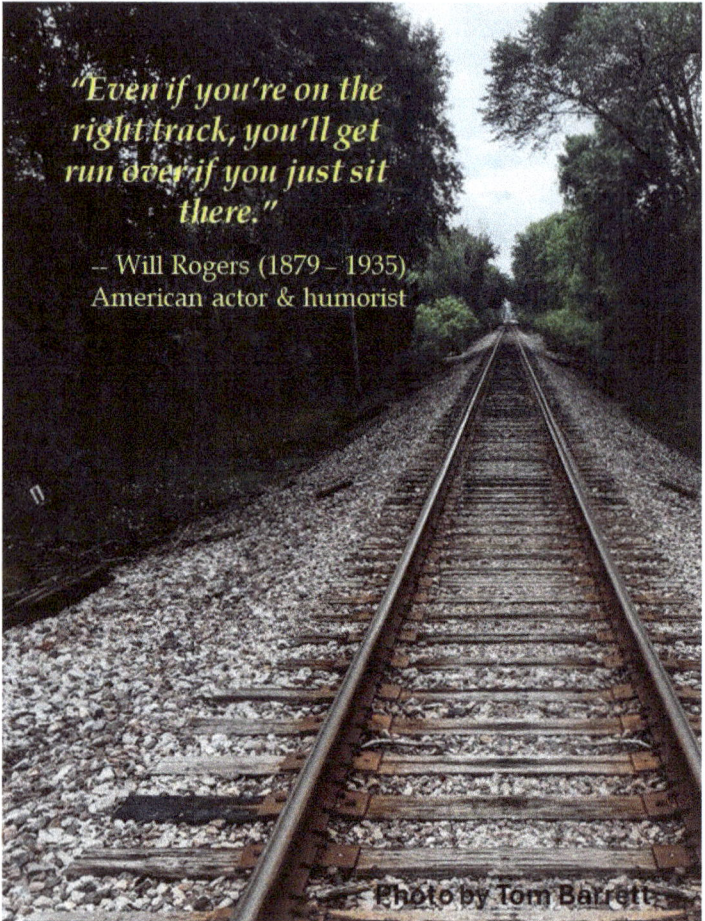

"Even if you're on the right track, you'll get run over if you just sit there."

-- Will Rogers (1879 – 1935)
American actor & humorist

Photo by Tom Barrett

"If you don't drive your business, you will be driven out of business."

--B. C. Forbes (1880 – 1954)
(Bertie Charles Forbes)
Scottish American financial journalist & author

"We are what we repeatedly do.
Excellence, therefore, is not an act but a habit."

-- Aristotle (384 BC – 322 BC)
Greek philosopher & polymath

"Destiny is not a matter of chance; it is a matter of choice. It is not to be waited for; it is to be achieved."

-- William Jennings Bryan (1860 – 1925)
American lawyer, orator, and politician

Photo by Mads Schmidt Rasmussen

Remember that internal factors also play leading roles in developing, shaping and shifting our various perspectives. We all have feelings, personalities, and different attitudes.

If we are healthy, our perspectives are apt to be quite different than if we are not well. We see things differently in daylight versus artificial light versus darkness.

Our moods impact our perspectives, too. We receive, handle, view, and analyze situations very differently when we are feeling happy and content versus when we are feeling sad, isolated, or angry.

Recognizing that we are never really alone is also helpful. We find genuine strength in numbers. That said, to be our best, we should be aware of the attitudes and perspectives of the people with whom we choose to surround ourselves.

We feel better, live better, and succeed better when we surround ourselves with positively enthusiastic people. We blossom more beautifully if the people we choose to have around us are assured, can-do people who share encouragement.

"Gettin' good players is easy.
Gettin' 'em to play together is the hard part."

--Casey Stengel (1890 – 1975)
American baseball player and manager

(Photo by Matteo Vistocco)

"None of us is as smart as all of us."

--Ken Blanchard (1939 -)
American author and business consultant

We do not have to "go it" alone. Our perspectives are far healthier when we are self-aware, open-hearted, and buoyed by positive associations.

Getting back up, dusting ourselves off, and starting all over again are words that most of us have needed to heed on many occasions. Life will knock us down. Not everything we attempt will bring immediate nor resounding success. What is important is trying again. And again. And again.

"Our greatest glory is not in never falling, but in rising every time we fall."

--Confucius (c 551 BC – 479 BC)
(born Kong Qiu)
Chinese philosopher

Sometimes we are strengthened in our endeavors by adding to or reshaping our perspectives. Reflecting on the paths we have followed and the beliefs we have held dear to get to a current spot is another important step.

We can widen our personal viewpoints by learning new perspectives. If we read, choose some different authors with different beliefs.

Or expose yourself to articles and other media sources than you might usually choose. We may not always like what we learn, but we are growing.

Learning how different concepts are developed and held by others strengthens us. It builds our knowledge. It can also powerfully strengthen our resolve, especially if we ultimately decide that someone else's outlook is not at all on the right track.

At the very least, learning different thoughts and interpretations helps us to better understand opposing perspectives, even if we choose not to personally subscribe to them. Only when we approach people with true compassion and empathy can we work past divisive differences.

(Photo by James Chan)

If someone berates us, scoffs at our beliefs, twists facts to suit their false narratives, or calls us nasty names, do not take it personally. They are merely revealing their own weakness, impassioned emotional state, insecurity, ignorance, and/or complete lack of compassion.

We must not sink to their level. They fear having their foundations shaken, as we all do. They are certainly not able to agree to disagree. They cannot turn the page.

Try not to take personally the harsh words and accusations that may fly our way when we have said something with which someone disagrees. Harsh judgments from strangers are easy to ignore, but when we feel slammed by someone who knows us and should know better, it hurts.

Crassly negative attitudes are carelessly negative attitudes. They hurt others, whether intentionally or not.

They are displayed in people who are, at least now, not open to learn anything different. So, there is little that can be shared with them that will even be seriously considered by them.

Thus, we focus on our own growth and the growth of people who do want a happier, more full existence. We reflect. We consider. We take action.

We seek new information. We actively learn about different perspectives. We challenge our own beliefs. We strengthen our confidence.

8

Practicing Mindfulness

Becoming meticulously mindful means carefully regarding our own thoughts, feelings, beliefs, and attitudes, as well as those held by others. We study and respect perspectives.

We exercise caution and great care in sharing our innermost dreams. We hold dear those we trust without question.

"It takes a lot of courage
to show your dreams to someone else."

-- Erma Bombeck (1927 – 1996)
American humorist

(Photo by Konrad Koller)

Living well requires great courage. We can all develop such strength. We can all increase our courage, confidence, and moral poise to move forward, always doing the very best we can.

We will make mistakes. If we are not making mistakes, then we are not fully living. Stepping outside of our comfort zones and trying new things brings greater fullness into our lives, despite some inevitable missteps along the way.

When we do make mistakes, we can and should make amends and start again. We stay active.

"I am grateful for all my problems.
I became stronger and
more able to meet those that were still to come."

-- James Cash Penney (1875 – 1971)
American businessman & entrepreneur
Founder of J.C. Penney in 1902

When life gets us down or seems to be making us crazy or nervous or concerned, there are positive steps we can take. Firstly, we can shift our focus.

Negative thoughts add stress. When we learn to focus on positives, we add powerful calmness to our survival arsenal.

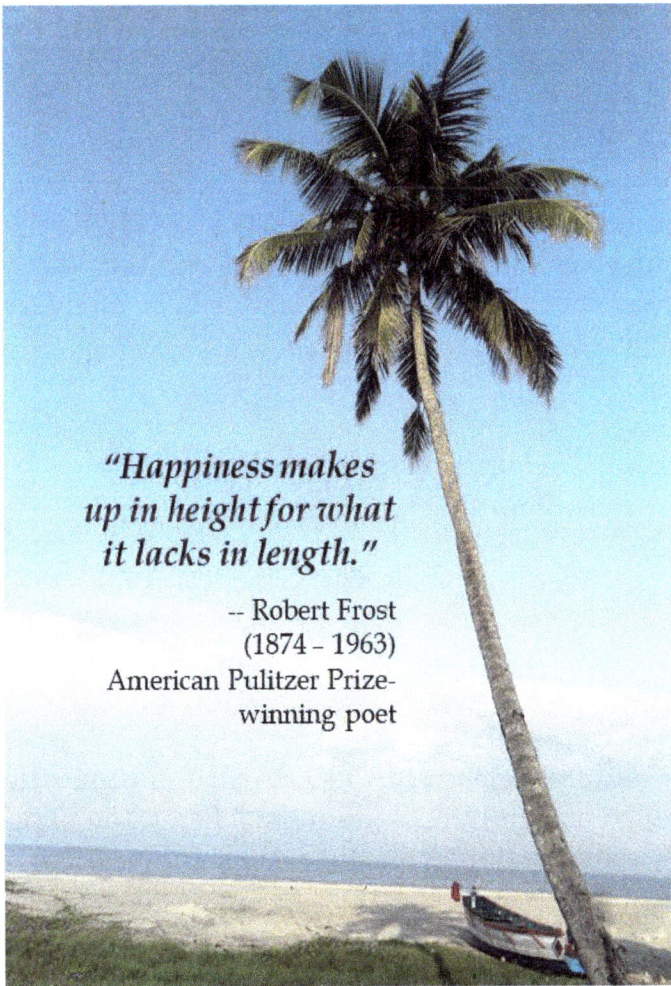

"Happiness makes
up in height for what
it lacks in length."

-- Robert Frost
(1874 - 1963)
American Pulitzer Prize-
winning poet

No matter how dreadful something may seem on the surface, try to seek "the good" in a situation. Yes, this can be very challenging.

Watching the news, for example, can drive us to feel a certain level of hopelessness and misery that no one needs in life. "If it bleeds, it leads" is a horrible and yet far too accurate accounting of the way many mainstream media outlets operate their news operations. Negative news draws in its audience and gets us hooked. We need to remind ourselves that 99% of what goes on every day is good, but the good deeds and events rarely get coverage.

"Many attempts to communicate are nullified by saying too much."

--Robert Greenleaf (1904 – 1990)
American business executive
& leadership consultant

We can also learn to practice what is commonly called an "attitude of gratitude." Reflect on things you are thankful for, which can shift our focus to the positive aspects of our life.

Some friends shared a clever technique with me. If a person says something negative about someone or insults them, then they must follow up by saying three nice things about that same person. Such practices may sound foolish, but they require us to pause and think beyond some immediate frustration.

*"It's not what you look at that matters.
It's what you see."*

--Henry David Thoreau (1817 – 1862)
American naturalist & writer

(Photo by Sally Williams)

*"You can't build a reputation
on what you're going to do."*

--Henry Ford (1863 – 1947)
American industrialist & business magnate
Founder of the Ford Motor Company

Action is a far cry from good intentions. We may have the very best intentions and yet fail to take that first step. We have to add action to reach our goals.

*"You may have to fight a battle
more than once to win."*

--Margaret Thatcher (1925 – 2013)
British stateswoman &
Prime Minister of the United Kingdom 1979 - 1990

We also should try to remember that we may not reach our goals on the first try. But stepping forward is important, despite the risks of sliding back. Even just taking two steps forward and one step backward is still forward progress.

Another helpful, though subtle action step is to not take ourselves too seriously. We are not perfect. We are people... imperfect people. God knows best; he did not arrange our anatomy in a way that makes it easy to pat ourselves on the back. This is good.

"We have not inherited the earth
from our ancestors;
we have only borrowed it from our children."

--Ancient Proverb

We can practice mindfulness and meditation. These help us detach from our negative thoughts and emotions, allowing us to appreciate some far more objective perspectives.

A simple way to disengage from negative mindsets is to engage in activities that promote well-being. These could include taking a break to exercise, spending some time in nature, or playing a little, enjoying a hobby that pleases you.

"Will you look back on life and say, 'I wish I had' or 'I'm glad I did'?"

-- Zig Ziglar (1926 – 2012)
American author, salesman, &
motivational speaker

Photo by Wallace Fonseca

Practicing patience and being persistent also become powerful perspective tools. Such skills seem to come naturally to some people, but for most of us, great attention and time are needed to make these skills regular parts of our lives.

Changing our perspective is a process. Sometimes it is a lengthy process. It is always an ongoing process. Feel confident in your chosen direction. Remember to be patient with yourself and celebrate small victories.

"Confidence is contagious."

--Vince Lombardi (1913 – 1970)
American NFL football coach

"Confidence is contagious.
So is lack of confidence."

--Michael O'Brien (1948 -)
Canadian author & artist

Listening to our thoughts helps us become more aware of our typical reactions and responses. If we find that we tend to track toward negativity, we can reframe our thinking.

When we recognize too much negativity in life and our personal thinking, we can follow some action steps to start reframing our thoughts to form a more positive approach. For example, when taking time to reflect, please be gentle with yourself and others. Make no accusations. Do no finger pointing. Just reflect.

Turn inner monologues into positives. Far too often we put ourselves down because we may have learned that it is easier to see ourselves as inferior or in error than to stand up to someone else who is expressing very strongly.

Sometimes we put others down because we do not understand their perspective or reasoning. We need to remember that we always benefit when we learn to stand in someone else's shoes, so to speak. We also grow when we assess toxic relationships.

Even when we are not able to physically separate ourselves from each and every one of these, we can insulate ourselves from their powerfully rancid attacks, insinuations, and negative impact.

When embracing change, it is also helpful to stop comparing ourselves with other people. Sadly, we humans tend to do this. Rarely do we see ourselves as worthy in comparison. In truth, we are far more worthy than we might dare to believe.

(Photo by Friedrich Frühling)

"The bravest are the most tender; the loving are the most daring."

-- Bayard Taylor (1825 - 1878)
American poet & literary critic

Photo by Kateryna Liznitsova

Another powerful part of practicing mindfulness is helping others. If you already do this, then you likely already have full awareness of the personal satisfaction that comes from giving someone else a hand up.

9

In Closing

We do get to choose our perspectives or how we view things. We can develop the ability to see the precious silver linings in even the darkest clouds. The flowers grow because the rain fell.

That light at the end of the tunnel is not usually an oncoming train. Sometimes it is some much-needed direction to finding our way.

(Photo by Sebastian Gabriel)

We may like our perspective. We may not. When we are exposed to new information or experiences, our brains form new neural pathways. These can alter our perceptions and ways of thinking.

Focusing our attention on different aspects of a situation or changing the way we process info can also cause perspective shifts. Always do this with the knowledge that we get to choose our own perspectives.

While we develop the ability to truly see things from a different perspective, we also build compassion and empathy toward others. We are opening doors and windows.

Photography Credits

Thank you to everyone who entrusted me with the use of their beautiful photographs.

Aziz Acharki	Konrad Koller
Meg Aghanyan	Chris Lawton
Danilo Alvesd	Rachel Ledford
Melissa Askew	Daniel Lincoln
Tom Barrett	Kateryna Liznitsova
Felipe Bastias	Sonny Maurico
Micah Bratt	Viktor Mindt
Renan Brun	Javid Naderi
James Chan	Mads Schmidt
Jonny Clow	Rasmussen
Creed Ferguson	Conny Schneider
Wallace Fonseca	Nadine E. Shaabana
Friedrich Frühling	Vicky Sim
Sebastian Gabriel	Gabriel Tenan
Scott Higdon	Matteo Vistocco
Zanyar Ibrahim	Klemen Vrankar
Steve Johnson	Sally Williams
Brett Jordan	Suzanne D. Williams

Special thanks to Johannes Plenio
for the cover photo.

About the Author

Cathy Burnham Martin's first published work came in elementary school when an early poem won a town library contest. That was back when her parents refused to let her have the then-popular "Chatty Cathy" doll, stating that one chatty Cathy in the house was more than enough. Though poetry took a back seat, she drove her writing and blabbing proficiencies along a highly eclectic career path through college recruitment, telecom marketing, corporate communications, TV broadcasting with an ABC affiliate, station management of an award-winning PEG-access station, bank organizing, and investor relations. An active board member and volunteer, she received Easter Seals' David P. Goodwin Lifetime Commitment Award. This professional voiceover artist, humorist, musical actress, journalist, and dedicated foodie earned numerous awards as a news anchor and businesswoman. She has produced and hosted groundbreaking documentaries, TV specials, and news reports, from the Moscow Superpower Summit and the opening of the Berlin Wall to coverage of Presidential Primaries. A born storyteller and business speaker, Cathy is a member of Actors Equity and writes daily articles for social media and the GoodLiving123.com website.

<u>Other Titles</u>

Life Seasonings Series:
  Hope

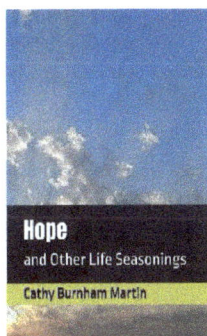

The Destiny trilogy:

  Destiny of Dreams… Time Is Dear

  Destiny of Determination… Faith and Family

  Destiny of Daring… Never Forget

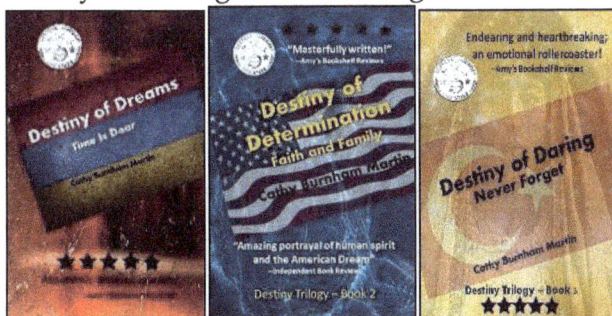

A Dangerous Book for Dogs:
   Train Your Humans with the Bandit Method

Dog Days in the Life of the Miles-Mannered Man

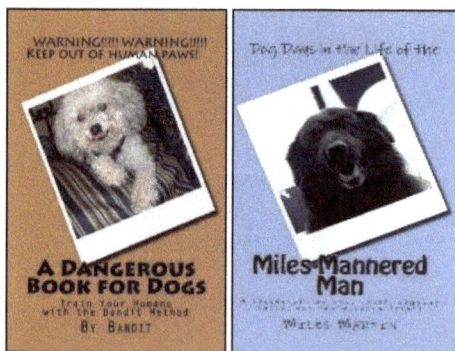

Healthy Thinking Habits:
   Seven Attitude Skills Simplified

Good Living Skills: Learned from My Mother

Encouragement: How to Be and Find Your Best

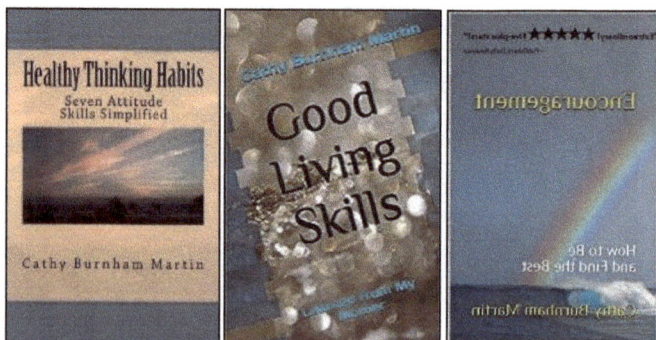

Of the Same Blood: Your Eurasian Heritage

The Ronald…
Daydreams, Wonderments & Other Ponderings

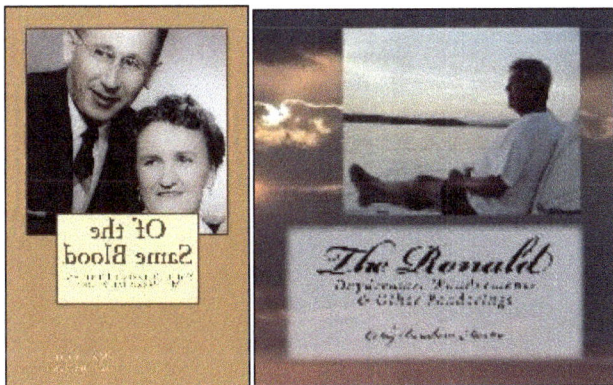

The Bimbo Has Brains… and Other Freaky Facts

The Bimbo Has MORE Brains…
Surviving Political Correctness

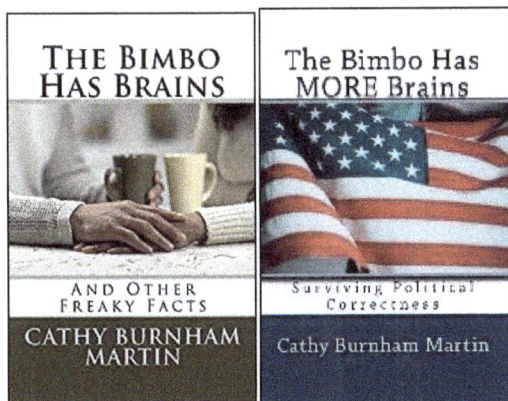

From the KISS Keep It Super Simple cookbooks:

50 Years of Fabulous Family Favorites

Sippers, Starters, and Sweets

Lunch, Brunch, and Entrees

Sides, Soup, Salad, Snacks, Etc.

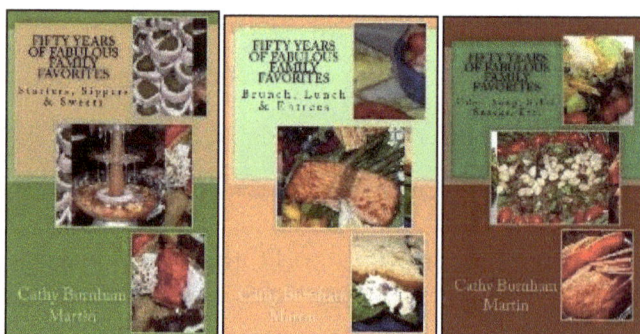

Champagne! Facts, Fizz, Food, & Fun

Cranberry Cooking

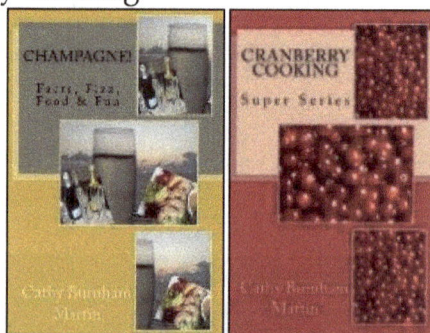

Dockside Dining: (series)

Round One

A Second Helping

Back for Thirds

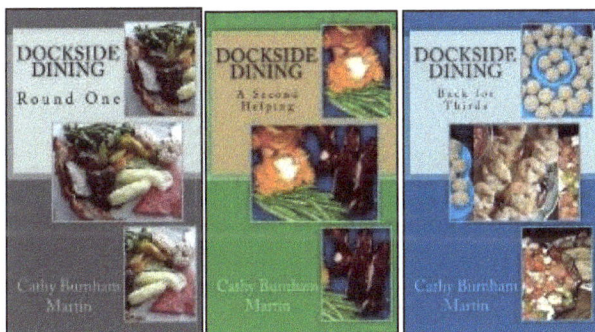

Lobacious Lobster…
Decadently Super Simple Recipes

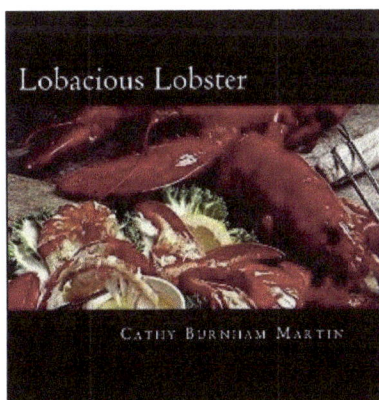

Find all books by Cathy Burnham Martin in paperback, digital, and audiobook formats anywhere books are sold and on her **www.GoodLiving123.com** site.

Partial List of Audiobooks Narrated by Cathy Burnham Martin

<u>Fiction</u>
Destiny Trilogy:
  Destiny of Dreams… Time Is Dear
    (Violent content warning)
  Destiny of Determination… Faith and Family
  Destiny of Daring… Never Forget
A Dangerous Book for Dogs…
  Train Your Humans with the Bandit Method
Kremlins Trilogy (Violent content warning)
    Citadels of Fire
    Bastions of Blood
    Dungeons of Destiny:
        An Epic Russian Historical Romance
Daniel's Fork: A Mystery Set in the
        Daniel's Fork Universe
            (Adult content warning)
The Relentless Brit

Non-Fiction
Encouragement: How to Be and Find the Best
Good Living Skills… Learned from My Mother
Healthy Thinking Habits:
        Seven Attitude Skills Simplified
The Bimbo Has Brains: And Other Freaky Facts
The Bimbo Has MORE Brains:
        Surviving Political Correctness
31 Days to a Stronger Marriage:
        A Guide to Building Closer Relationships
Exploring Past Lives: A Guide to the Soul's Travels
Why We Fail in Love: A Study into the Pursuit of
        One of Mankind's Most Precious Desires
The Hormone Fix: Naturally Rebalance Your System
        in 10 Weeks

www.ingramcontent.com/pod-product-compliance
Lightning Source LLC
Chambersburg PA
CBHW071620040426
42452CB00009B/1406